Horatio Hale

The Origin of Languages and the Antiquity of Speaking Man

An address before the Section of anthropology of the American

association for the advancement of science, at Buffalo, August, 1886

Horatio Hale

The Origin of Languages and the Antiquity of Speaking Man
An address before the Section of anthropology of the American association for the advancement of science, at Buffalo, August, 1886

ISBN/EAN: 9783337255312

Printed in Europe, USA, Canada, Australia, Japan

Cover: Foto ©Andreas Hilbeck / pixelio.de

More available books at **www.hansebooks.com**

THE

ORIGIN OF LANGUAGES,

AND THE

ANTIQUITY OF SPEAKING MAN.

AN ADDRESS

BEFORE THE SECTION OF ANTHROPOLOGY OF THE AMERICAN
ASSOCIATION FOR THE ADVANCEMENT OF SCIENCE,

AT BUFFALO, AUGUST, 1886.

By HORATIO HALE,

VICE-PRESIDENT.

[From the Proceedings of the American Association for the Advancement
of Science, Vol. XXXV.]

CAMBRIDGE:
JOHN WILSON AND SON.
University Press.
1886.

ADDRESS

BY

HORATIO HALE,

VICE-PRESIDENT, SECTION H.

---

*THE ORIGIN OF LANGUAGES, AND THE ANTIQUITY OF
SPEAKING MAN.*

In the study of every science there arise from time to time
difficult questions or problems, which seem to bar the way of the
student in one direction or another. It becomes apparent that on
the proper solution of these problems the progress of the science
mainly depends ; and the minds of all inquirers are bent earnestly
on the discovery of this solution. Such in biology are the questions
of the origin of life and the genesis of species. Anthropology, and
its auxiliary or component sciences of comparative philology, ethnology, and archæology, have their share of these problems. Among
them two of the most important are undoubtedly, in philology, the
question of the origin of linguistic stocks, and in archæology, the
question of the epoch at which man acquired the faculty of speech.
In the language of modern diplomacy, these would be styled
" burning questions," which must be settled before any hopeful
progress can be made in other discussions. A brief consideration
of these questions, in the light cast upon them by the most recent
discoveries, may therefore be deemed to form an appropriate
introduction to the work of our Section. Briefly defined, then, our
inquiry on this occasion will have for its subjects, or rather its
subject, — for the two questions are closely connected, and form in
reality but one problem, — the origin of languages and the antiquity
of speaking man.

The question of the origin of languages must be distinguished
from the different and larger question of the origin of language,

which belongs rather to anthropology proper than to the science of linguistics, and will come under consideration in the later part of our inquiry. Nor yet does our question concern the rise and development of the different tongues belonging to one linguistic stock or family, like the sixty languages of the Aryan or Indo-European stock, the twenty languages of the Hamito-Semitic family, the one hundred and sixty-eight languages enumerated by Mr. R. N. Cust as composing the great Bantu or South African family, and the thirty-five languages of the wide-spread Algonkin stock. Such idioms, however much they may differ, are in their nature only dialects. The manner in which these idioms originate is perfectly well understood. When two communities, in the barbarous or semi-barbarous stage, whose members spoke originally the same language, have been separated for a certain length of time, a difference of dialect, due to differences of climate, culture, customs, and other circumstances, grows up between them. They can still understand each other's speech, but there are variances in pronunciation and in the use of certain words, by which they can readily be distinguished. In the progress of time these differences increase. Grammatical peculiarities are developed. Permutations of elementary sounds, like those which are manifested in the famous "Grimm's law," alter whole classes of words beyond the recognition of a hearer familiar only with the original speech. And, finally, two distinct languages are found to have come into being, so diverse in vocabulary and grammar that each must be learned as a foreign speech by the speakers of the other tongue. Yet, however wide may be the diversity, a careful analysis and comparison will always disclose the kinship, and indicate the common origin of the two languages.

But while the manner in which different languages of the same family arise is thus evident enough, not merely in theory, but in the numerous instances which have occurred within historic times, we have neither instance nor satisfactory theory to explain the distinction between the families themselves. When, for example, we have traced back the Aryan (or Indo-European) languages and the Semitic languages to their separate mother-tongues, which we are able to frame out of the scattered dialects, we find between these two mother-tongues a great gulf, which no explanation thus far proposed has sufficed to bridge over. How strongly the sense of this difficulty has been felt by the highest minds engaged in philological study will be evident from two striking examples. Sixty years ago, Baron William von Humboldt, who held in this branch of study the same position which was held by his illustrious brother in the natural sciences, found it—as Dr. Brinton states in the excellent Introduction to his translation of Humboldt's "Philosophic Grammar of the American Languages"—"so contrary to the results of his prolonged and profound study of languages to believe, for instance, that a tongue like the Sanscrit could ever be developed from one like the Chinese, that he frankly said that he would rather accept at once the doctrine of those who attribute the different idioms of men to an immediate revelation from God." Fifty years later, the distinguished representative of linguistic science in France, Professor Abel Hovelacque, pronounced in his admirable compendium, "La Linguistique" (1875), what may be deemed the "last word" of science on this subject. "Not only," he affirms, "is there no grammatical identity between the system of the Semitic languages and that of the Indo-European tongues, but these two comprehend inflection in a manner entirely different. Their roots are totally distinct; their formative elements are essentially different; and there is no relation between the two modes in which these elements perform their functions. The abyss between the two systems is not merely profound, — it is impassable."

Such then is the difficulty and the gravity of this question of the origin of languages, — a problem as serious and as fundamentally important for philological science as the question of the origin of species is deemed in biology; and, as has been already remarked, on the correct solution of this problem the progress and the future, not merely of philology, but of the whole "Science of Man," may be said to depend. For not until it is finally settled will the minds of the students of this science be in accord on the all-important question whether the human race belongs to many species or to only one.

Attempts to solve the problem have not been lacking. Several solutions have, indeed, been proposed, but no one of them has met with general acceptance. One of these suggested explanations takes into account the element of time. If man has existed for thousands of centuries, his speech might, it is supposed, have undergone in that vast period all the alterations required to produce these various linguistic stocks. But the conclusions of William von Humboldt and of Professor Hovelacque, already cited, — conclusions which express the generally received views of the best philologists, — show that this explanation cannot be entertained. If the development of a language like the Sanscrit from a language like the Chinese is inconceivable, — if the abyss between the Semitic and the Indo-European tongues is impassable, — then it is clear that the mere element of time cannot help us in this difficulty. Moreover, we know, as a matter of fact, that the passage of time has not the effect supposed. It is certain that the distance between a Semitic tongue and an Aryan tongue in our day — as, for example, between the modern Arabic and the English — is no greater and no less than was the distance between the Semitic Assyrian and the Aryan Sanscrit a thousand years before the Christian era. If thirty centuries have made no appreciable change in the distinction between these two linguistic families, why should we suppose that three thousand centuries would produce any effect in that direction? But in reality, as will be seen in the progress of our inquiry, it is most probable that no such element of long-protracted time can be admitted in the present case.

Another theory which has been favored by some esteemed writers, and among others by Lyell in his famous work on the " Antiquity of Man," supposes that, when men first acquired the capacity of speech, their use of language was probably confined to a few monosyllabic roots, of vague and fluctuating import, and that, when those who spoke this primitive and half-formed tongue were scattered abroad, their imperfect speech developed into the widely different languages which became the mother-tongues of the various linguistic families. This ingenious hypothesis, however, is liable, as will be seen, to all the objections which the previously described theory has had to encounter, and, like that, does not stand the test either of reasoning or of facts. If those who used this primitive speech were — as we must suppose them to have been — human beings like those who now exist, their language was a language complete in all its parts ; for no tribe of men has been found in any part of the world so low in the scale of humanity as not to have a complete and thoroughly organized language. This language may, like the Chinese and the Anamese, consist wholly or mainly of roots ; but it is none the less complete, and — what is more important to the argument — none the less permanent. In the vast Chinese empire, after an existence of more than four thousand years, one spoken language prevails, with differences of dialect not so great as the differences which exist between the Romanic languages of

Europe. If it be suggested that this permanence may be due to the existence of one government and of a written character, the same cannot be affirmed of the many monosyllabic languages belonging to the great linguistic families of Transgangetic India, — the Tibeto-Burman family, the Tai family, and the Mon-Anam family, — where sometimes, as is shown by Mr. Cust in his valuable work on the "Modern Languages of the East Indies," twenty different languages belonging to one linguistic stock are spoken by communities living under a dozen different governments, and in every stage of culture. Furthermore, it may be asked, How is it possible to suppose that the nineteen distinct linguistic stocks which have been found to exist in what is now the State of California can have originated in dialects of a monosyllabic language spoken thousands of years ago on another continent? Where did these dialects lose all traces of resemblance, and how did the speakers of them come to be living side by side in this narrow area? This theory, it will be seen, raises difficulties far greater than those which it undertakes to explain.

Finally, the latest proposed solution, and one which merits special attention for its scientific interest and the weight of authority in its favor, is the theory first propounded, I believe, by the distinguished Viennese ethnologist, Dr. Frederick Müller, and adopted by Dr. Ernest Haeckel, by Professor Hovelacque, by General Faidherbe, and other eminent authorities. This theory supposes that men, or rather the precursors of man, were at first incapable of speech, and that they acquired this capacity at different places. This opinion is so important that it should be stated in the language of one of its chief advocates. In his work, "La Linguistique," already quoted, Professor Hovelacque, after describing the impassable gulf which separates the Semitic and the Indo-European languages, adds that the case of these languages is the case of a considerable number of linguistic systems ; and he proceeds : "The consequence of this fact is important. If, as we have shown, the faculty of articulate speech is the proper and the sole characteristic of man, and if the different linguistic systems, which we know, are irreducible, they must have come into existence separately, in regions entirely distinct. It follows that the precursor of man, the first to acquire the faculty of articulate language, has gained this faculty in different places at the same time, and has thus given birth to many human races originally distinct."

Dr. Frederick Müller, whose noble work, "The Outline of Linguistic Science " (*Grundriss der Sprachwissenschaft*), is for students of our time what the " Mithridates " of Adelung and Vater was to those of a former generation, — the great thesaurus of philologic research and analysis, — not only maintains this view, but lays down specifically the divisions of race into which the speechless descendants of the primitive precursor of our kind — the *homo primigenius alalus* — had separated before they acquired the faculty of language. Yet, notwithstanding the weight which may be justly given to the opinions of such high authorities, it may be affirmed in this case, as in the case of the earlier theories, that the difficulties raised by the hypothesis are immeasurably greater than those which it is designed to remove.

The number of totally different linguistic stocks, so far as now known, is at the lowest computation over two hundred; and 'of these the greater portion belong to the western continent. The theory now under consideration supposes that both continents were in early times inhabited throughout by beings resembling men, but incapable of speech. It is evident that the process of this wide dispersion of beings in that semi-brutal condition must have occupied a vast space of time. We are required to believe that suddenly and separately, with no common impulse or cause, but at one time, all these scattered tribes, which had existed for countless ages without language, fortuitously acquired the faculty of speech, invented each its own language, and began to converse. Such a stupendous event — the simultaneous acquisition, by more than two hundred distinct communities of speechless beings, of the faculty which specially distinguishes man from the brute — would well deserve to be styled miraculous.

To come down to specific particulars, — many years ago, in making the first ethnographical survey of Oregon, I found that there were in that region no less than twelve linguistic stocks, — that is, families of languages as distinct from one another in words and grammar as the Semitic family is from the Indo-European. The able linguists of the Bureau of Ethnology, Messrs. Gatschet and Dorsey, have made further investigations in this region, and have visited portions of it which I was unable to reach. Their researches have confirmed my classification, and have added two or three additional stocks. South of this district, Mr. Stephen Powers, in his excellent Report on California, published by the same Bureau, has continued the survey in that direction, and has found sixteen additional linguistic stocks (besides three of the Oregon stocks) within the limits of that State. Thus, in a region not much larger than France, we find at least thirty distinct families of languages existing together. We are expected to believe that thirty separate communities of speechless precursors of men, after living side by side in this inarticulate condition for an indefinite period, suddenly and simultaneously acquired the power of speech, and began at once to talk in thirty distinct languages. The mere statement of this grotesque proposition seems sufficient to refute it.

While some of the ablest reasoners have thus been groping vaguely and blindly, in wrong directions, for the solution of this problem, and while others, like Humboldt and Whitney, have given it up in despair, the simple and sufficient explanation has been lying close at hand, awaiting only, like many other discoveries in science, the observation of some facts of common occurrence to bring it to light. In the present case, the two observers who have made the conclusive facts known to us have both been Americans, and both of them writers of more than ordinary intelligence; but both were entirely unknown in this branch of investigation, and both, moreover, had the singular ill-fortune of publishing their observations in works of such limited circulation that their important contributions to science have hitherto failed to attain the notice they deserved. Their observations were made at about the same time, nearly twenty years ago, but published at different dates, — the first in 1868, the second ten years later. It was the latter publication which first attracted my attention, soon after its appearance, and led to a course of study and inquiry resulting in the facts and conclusions now to be detailed.

Before setting forth the facts, it will be well to state at once the result of the inquiry. Briefly, then, the plain conclusion to which all the observations point with irresistible force is, that the origin of linguistic stocks is to be found in what may be termed the language-making instinct of very young children. From numerous cases, of which the history has been traced, it appears that, when two children who are just beginning to speak are left much together, they sometimes invent a complete language, sufficient for all purposes of mutual intercourse, and yet totally unintelligible to their parents and others about them. It is evident that, in an ordinary household, the conditions under which such a language would be formed are most likely to occur in the case of twins. One of the most remarkable instances is that of which a record has been preserved in one of the publications to which reference has been made. This is a volume, published in 1878, by Miss E. H. Watson, a lady of Boston, the authoress of several esteemed works on historical subjects. In performing the pious duty of giving to the world an essay by her father, the late George Watson, on "The Structure of Language, and the Uniform Notation and Classification of Vowels for all Languages," the editress has prefixed to it two essays of her own, on "The Origin of Language," and on "Spelling Reform," which show evidence of much reading and thought, and contain many valuable suggestions. The volume bears the peculiar title, apparently adopted by Mr. Watson, of "The Universe of Language," and appeared under the auspices of the now defunct "Authors' Publishing Company," by whose lapse most of the edition was cast back upon the hands of the editress, and thus failed to obtain the attention and credit which its value should have insured.

The first of Miss Watson's essays in this volume comprises, in especial, one contribution to scientific knowledge, — her account of the "children's language," — which she justly deemed to be of great value, and which is perhaps even more important than she supposed. It is presented by her as bearing upon the question of the origin of human speech. While it has undoubtedly a real interest in this respect, its main value resides in the light which it casts on the origin of linguistic stocks. There is nothing in the example which clearly proves that the children in question would have spoken at all if they had not heard their parents and others about them communicating by oral sounds, — though we may, on good grounds (as will be shown), believe that they would have done so. What the case really establishes is, that children who have thus learned to speak may invent a language of their own, different from all that they hear around them, and yet adequate to all the purposes of speech.

In the year 1860 two children, twin boys, were born in a respectable family residing in a suburb of Boston. They were in part of German descent, their mother's father having come from Germany to America at the age of seventeen ; but the German language, we are told, was never spoken in the household. The children were so closely alike that their grandmother, who often came to see them, could only distinguish them by some colored string or ribbon tied around the arm. As often happens in such cases, an intense affection existed between them, and they were constantly together. The remainder of their interesting story will be best told in the words of the writer, to whose enlightened zeal for science we are indebted for our knowledge of the facts. She thus relates it : —

" At the usual age these twins began to talk, but, strange to say, *not* their ' mother-tongue.' They had a language of their own, and no pains could induce them to speak anything else. It was in vain that a little sister, five years older than they, tried to make them speak their *native language*, — as it would have been. They persistently refused to utter a syllable of English. Not even the usual first words, ' papa,' ' mamma,' ' father,' ' mother,' it is said, did they ever speak ; and, said the lady who gave this information to the writer, — who was an aunt of the children, and whose home was with them, — they were never known during this interval to call their mother by that name. They had their own name for her, but never the English. In fact, though they had the usual affections, were rejoiced to see their father at his returning home each night, playing with him, etc., they would seem to have been otherwise completely taken up, absorbed with each other. . . . The children had not yet been to school ; for, not being able to speak their ' own English,' it seemed impossible to send them from home. They thus passed the days, playing and talking together in their own speech, with all the liveliness and volubility of common children. Their accent was *German*, — as it seemed to the family. They had regular words, a few of which the family learned sometimes to distinguish ; as that, for example, for carriage, which, on hearing one pass in the street, they would exclaim out, and run to the window."

This word for carriage, we are told in another place, was *nī-si-boo-a*, of which, it is added, the syllables were sometimes so repeated that they made a much longer word. This, unfortunately, is the only word of the language which Miss Watson was able to ascertain ; but even from this one example some interesting inferences may be drawn. The speech was plainly not monosyllabic ; and the word in question is neither English nor German. In the concluding syllables, if lengthened by repetition, we may perhaps discern an attempt to imitate the rumbling of a carriage. " The children," we are told, " went in the family by the name of the little ' Dutch boys'; and the father, at first inquiry of the writer, called their speech 'a mixture of German and English.' But the children at that time had never heard any German spoken; therefore it could not have been the former; and if some English words were picked up — as would be but probable — they seem to have been so transformed that they were not recognizable as such, unless rarely. . . . The mother relates that, although she could not understand their language, she contrived, by attention, to discover what they wished or meant."

If the quick ear of a mother, after years of intercourse, could not discern the English words, it is clear that they were not used in a form which would have properly entitled them to that name. The important information is added, that, "even in that early stage, the language was complete and full; that is, it was all that was needed. The children were at no loss to express themselves in their plays, their 'chatterings' with each other, as our informant expressed it, all day. Indeed, the writer would gather from the description given that they were more than usually animated between themselves."

The sequel of the story, as graphically told by the authoress, has an interest, as showing that the language spoken around these children was to them really a foreign speech. "It finally seeming hopeless that they were going to learn their 'own tongue,' as we call it, it was concluded to send them to school in the neighborhood, they being now six or seven years old. For a week, as the lady teacher described to whom they were sent, they were perfectly mute; not a sound could be heard from them, but they sat with their eyes intently fixed upon the children, seeming to be watching their every motion, — and, no doubt, listening to every sound. At the end of that time they were induced to utter some words, and gradually and naturally they began, for the first time, to learn their 'native English.' With this accomplishment, the other began, also naturally, to fade away, until the memory, with the use of it, passed from their mind."

We cannot but share in the regret expressed by the accomplished authoress that she was not acquainted with these facts until it was too late to preserve a record of the language itself, which, it is evident, would have been of great scientific interest. Indeed, but for the facts now to be related, a suspicion might naturally remain, in spite of all that is said of the total strangeness of the children's speech, that it was, after all, only an exaggerated specimen of ordinary "baby-talk," — a mere babble of imperfect English, mixed with some mimicries of natural sounds. Most fortunately, another example affords the precise evidence required to dispel all such suspicion. Though in the case now to be described the circumstances were somewhat different, and the language was probably less complete than in the instance just recorded, yet it happened, by good fortune, that a careful and scientific observer was in a position to preserve at least a portion of it for our information. While these interesting twins were chattering their peculiar language in Boston, a little four-year-old girl and her younger brother in Albany were perplexing their parents by a similar vagary. A clear and satisfactory account of this phenomenon was given by the late E. R. Hun, M.D., of that city, in an article published in the Monthly Journal of Psychological Medicine (in the volume for 1868), under the title of "Singular Development of Language in a Child." For my knowledge of this most important evidence, as well as for many other valuable suggestions, I have to thank our distinguished associate, Dr. Brinton, whose attention no essential fact relating to his favorite sciences is likely to escape.

The statements with which Dr. Hun commences his account are too succinct to be abridged. "The subject of this observation," he writes, "is a girl aged four and a half years, sprightly, intelligent, and in good health. The mother observed, when she was two years old, that she was backward in speaking, and only used the words 'papa' and 'mamma.' After that she began to use words of her own invention, and though she understood readily what was said, never employed the words used by others. Gradually she enlarged her vocabulary until it has reached the extent described below. She has a brother eighteen months younger than herself, who has learned her language, so that they talk freely together. He, however, seems to have adopted it only because he has more intercourse with her than with others; and in some instances he will use a proper word with his mother, and his sister's word with her. She, however, persists in using only her own words, though her parents, who are uneasy about her peculiarity of speech, make great efforts to induce her to use proper words. As to the possibility of her having learned these words from others, it is proper to state that her parents are persons of cultivation, who use only the English language. The mother has learned

French, but never uses the language in conversation. The domestics, as well as the nurses, speak English without any peculiarities, and the child has heard even less than usual of what is called baby-talk. Some of the words and phrases have a resemblance to the French; but it is certain that no person using that language has frequented the house, and it is doubtful whether the child has on any occasion heard it spoken. There seems to be no difficulty about the vocal organs. She uses her language readily and freely, and when she is with her brother they converse with great rapidity and fluency."

Dr. Hun then gives the vocabulary, which, he states, was such as he had " been able at different times to compile from the child herself, and especially from the report of her mother." From this statement we may infer that the list probably did not include the whole number of words in this child-language. It comprises, in fact, only twenty-one distinct words, though many of these were used in a great variety of acceptations, indicated by the order in which they were arranged, or by compounding them in various ways. As we know, however, on excellent authority, that the conversation of English laborers has been found to be carried on with no more than a hundred words, we may believe that the talk of the children might be fluent enough with a much more limited vocabulary. " I once listened," — writes Archdeacon Farrar, in his work on " Language and Languages," — " for a long time together to the conversation of three peasants who were gathering apples among the boughs of an orchard, and, as far as I could conjecture, the whole number of words they used did not exceed a hundred ; the same word was made to serve a variety of purposes." This, it will be seen, was exactly the case with the language of these children.

Three or four of the words, as Dr. Hun remarks, bear an evident resemblance to the French, and others might, by a slight change, be traced to that language. He was unable, it will be seen, to say positively that the girl had never heard the language spoken ; and it seems not unlikely that, if not among the domestics, at least among the persons who visited them, there may have been one who amused herself, innocently enough, by teaching the child a few words of that tongue. It is, indeed, by no means improbable that the peculiar linguistic instinct may thus have been first aroused in the mind of the girl, when just beginning to speak. Among the words showing this resemblance are *feu* (pronounced, we are expressly told, like the French word), used to signify "fire, light, cigar, sun"; *too* (the French *tout*), meaning "all, everything"; and *ne pa* (whether pronounced as in French, or otherwise, we are not told), signifying "not." *Petee-petee*, the name given to the boy by his sister, is apparently the French *petit*, little; and *ma*, I, may be from the French *moi*, me. If, however, the child was really able to catch and remember so readily these foreign sounds at such an early age, and to interweave them into a speech of her own, it would merely show how readily and strongly in her case the language-making faculty was developed.

Of words formed by imitation of sounds, the language shows barely a trace. The mewing of the cat evidently suggested the word *mea*, which signified both cat and furs. For the other vocables which make up this speech, no origin can be conjectured. We can merely notice that in some of the words the liking which children and some races of men have for the repetition of sounds is apparent. Thus we have *migno-migno*, signifying "water, wash, bath"; *go-go*, "delicacies, as sugar, candy, or dessert"; and *waia-waiar*, "black, darkness, or a negro." There is, as will be seen from these examples, no special tendency to the monosyllabic form. *Gummigar*, we are told, signifies "all the substantials of the table, such as bread, meat, vegetables, etc."; and the same word is used to designate the cook. The boy, it is added, does not use this word, but uses *gna-migna*, which the girl considers a mistake. From which we may gather that even at that tender age the form of their language had become with them an object of thought; and we may infer, moreover, that the language was not invented solely by the girl, but that both the children contributed to frame it.

Of miscellaneous words may be mentioned *gar*, "horse"; *deer*, "money of any kind"; *beer*, "literature, books, or school"; *peer*, "ball"; *bau*, "soldier, music"; *odo*, "to send for, to go out, to take away"; *keh*, "to soil"; *pa-ma*, "to go to sleep, pillow, bed." The variety of acceptations which each word was capable of receiving is exemplified in many ways. Thus *feu* might become an adjective, as *ne-pa feu*, "not warm." The verb *odo* had many meanings, according to its position or the words which accompanied it. *Ma odo*, "I (want to) go out"; *gar odo*, "send for the horse"; *too odo*, "all gone." *Gaän* signified God; and we are told, "When it rains, the children often run to the window, and call out, *Gaän odo migno-migno, feu odo*, which means, 'God take away the rain, and send the sun'; *odo* before the object meaning 'to take away,' and after the object, 'to send.'" From this remark and example we learn, not merely that the language had — as all real languages must have — its rules of construction, but that these were sometimes different from the English rules. This also appears in the form *mea waia-waiar*, "dark furs" (literally, "furs dark"), where the adjective follows its substantive.

The odd and unexpected associations which in all languages govern the meaning of words are apparent in this brief vocabulary. We can gather from it that the parents were Catholics, and punctual in church observances. The words *papa* and *mamma* were used separately in their ordinary sense; but when linked together in the compound term *papa-mamma*, they signified (according to the connection, we may presume) "church, prayerbook, cross, priest, to say their prayers." *Bau* was "soldier"; but, we are told, from seeing the bishop in his mitre and vestments, thinking he was a soldier, they applied the word *bau* to him. *Gar odo* properly signified "send for the horse"; but as the children frequently saw their father, when a carriage was wanted, write an order and send it to the stable, they came to use the same expression (*gar odo*) for pencil and paper.

There is no appearance of inflection, properly speaking, in the language; and this is only what might be expected. Very young children rarely use inflected forms in any language. The English child of three or four years says, "Mary cup," for "Mary's cup"; and "Dog bite Harry" will represent every tense and mood. It is by no means improbable that, if the children had continued to use their own language for a few years longer, inflections would have been developed in it, as we see that peculiar forms of construction and novel compounds — which are the germs of inflection — had already made their appearance.

These two recorded instances of child-languages have led to further inquiries, which, though pursued only for a brief period, and in a limited field, have shown that cases of this sort are by no means uncommon. An esteemed physician of my acquaintance, whose childhood was passed in the city of Kingston, Ontario, has informed me of a case within his own knowledge which bears a remarkable resemblance to that of the Albany children. It occurred in that city nearly thirty years ago, when my informant was about seven years old ; but his recollection of it is perfectly distinct. A widower with several children, one of whom was a boy between four and five years old, married a widow with a single child, — a girl, somewhat younger than the boy. They lived directly opposite the residence of my friend's parents, and he knew the children intimately. The boy was unusually backward in his speech, and at the time of the marriage spoke imperfectly. He and the little girl soon became inseparable playmates, and formed a language of their own, which was unintelligible to their parents and friends. They had names of their own invention for all the objects about them, and must have had a corresponding supply of verbs and other parts of speech, as their talk was fluent and incessant. My informant, with his brother and the other children who lived near them, often listened to this chatter with great amusement, and came at last to recognize a number of the most common expressions. The only one which he can now remember was the word for cat, which fastened itself in his mind by its oddity. The little philologists had a favorite cat, which they often held aloft for the admiration of the spectators across the street, shouting to them its extraordinary name of *shindikik*. This term, like the solitary word preserved of the speech of the Boston children, proves at least that the language had passed beyond the infantile or Chinese stage, when every word is a monosyllable, usually ending in a vowel. The mother of the little girl became at length so much disquieted by the persistency of the children in refusing to speak English, that she finally resorted to the expedient of separating them, and placed the daughter for a time under the care of a relative residing at a distance. The children soon forgot their abnormal speech, and, as both the parents are dead, it is not likely that any more relics of it will be recovered.

How soon such memories fade from the minds of both speakers and hearers, and how little attention such incidents attract, is shown by another case, which occurred some twenty years ago in the family of one of my nearest neighbors and friends, but was so little noticed that I had never heard of it until the present year. In this family the two youngest children — a boy and a girl — were twins, and as usually happens, were left much together. When they were three or four years old they were accustomed, as their elder sister informs me, to talk together in a language which no one else understood. The other members of the family called it

their " gibberish," but otherwise paid little attention to it. The
father would sometimes say, " Hear those children chattering ! "
and the other members of the family would listen, and smile at the
stream of unintelligible sounds. The twins were wont to climb into
their father's carriage in the stable, and " chatter away," as my informant says, for hours in this strange language. Their sister
remembers that it sounded as though the words were quite short.
But the single word which survives in the family recollection is a
dissyllable, — the word for milk, which was *cully.* The little girl
accompanied her speech with gestures, but the boy did not. As
they grew older, they gradually gave up their peculiar speech. The
boy is dead. The girl, now an intelligent and accomplished young
lady, has totally forgotten the words of their childish speech, though
she remembers well the fact of using it and the amusement it ex-
cited. She remembers also that the others spoke of them as " talking Scotch," or " in Scotch fashion." Their father, a well-educated
professional gentleman, was of Scottish birth, but had lived much
in England ; and neither he nor any of the children had any marked
accent differing from that of ordinary English speech.

A case which recalls that of the Boston boys is related to me by
a lady friend who was educated in Toronto. She remembers perfectly well the amusement caused, in the school which she attended
in her early childhood, by two little boys, sons of a wealthy gentleman of that city, who were accustomed to converse together in a
language of their own. Their ages were about five or six, one
being somewhat more than a year older than the other. The
youngest, however, was slightly the taller of the two. They were
fine, intelligent boys, and were always together, both at home and
in the school. My informant knew the family, which was a rather
large one, — five boys and a girl. These children were left much
to themselves, and had a language of their own, in which they
always conversed. The other children in the school used to listen
to them as they chattered together, and laugh heartily at the
strange speech of which they could not understand a word. The
boys spoke English with difficulty, and very imperfectly, like persons struggling to express their ideas in a foreign tongue. In
speaking it, they had to eke out their words with many gestures
and signs to make themselves understood ; but in talking together
in their own language, they used no gestures, and spoke very
fluently. She remembers that the words which they used seemed

quite short. In imitating from memory their mode of speech she uses monosyllables. They had a nurse, an intelligent middle-aged woman, who brought them to the school in the morning, and came for them in the afternoon. She had had the care of them from infancy, and understood their language, but did not speak it. She was accustomed to speak to them in English, and they would reply to her in their own tongue. They learned but little at the school, and had apparently been sent there chiefly to accustom them to be with children of their own age, and to learn to speak like them. My friend knew them in after life, as grown-up young men, when they spoke English like other people.

But it is needless to multiply examples. The instances thus recorded do not by any means exhaust the list. I have not yet had the fortunate opportunity — which Dr. Hun enjoyed and used to such good advantage — of personally hearing and investigating such a child-language. But as it is evident that its development is not a fact of very rare occurrence, we may hope, now that attention has been drawn to the matter, that this interesting subject of inquiry will soon be thoroughly studied by competent observers. These cases, it must be remembered, are, after all, merely intensified forms of a phenomenon which is of constant recurrence. The inclination of very young children to employ words and forms of speech of their own is well known, though it is only under peculiar circumstances that this language acquires the extent and the permanence which it attained in the cases now recorded. Along with this inclination of children, a corresponding disposition of their elders in conversing with them will be noticed. The "baby-talk" in which mothers and nurses in all communities, civilized and savage, are wont to indulge, is in some respects totally distinct from their ordinary speech. It is utterly devoid of inflections, of articles, and of pronouns, has its own pronunciation, its own syntax and construction, and many peculiar words. The importance of this baby-talk as an element of linguistic science has been recognized by eminent scientific investigators. Dr. Tylor, in the fifth chapter of his work on "Primitive Culture," touches upon this subject with some noteworthy remarks and suggestions, of which the general tenor is strikingly confirmed by the speech of the Albany children. "Children's language," he observes, "may give a valuable lesson to the philologist." After quoting many examples of infantile words in use in various countries, he adds: "In this language, the theory of root-sounds fairly breaks down." "It is obvious," he continues, "that the leading principle of their formation is, not to adopt words distinguished by the expressive character of their sound, but to choose somehow a fixed word to answer a given purpose." So Mr. George P. Marsh, in his "Lectures on the English Language," remarks, that the question whether the power of speech is a faculty or an art may be answered, "in a general way, by saying that the use of articulate language is a faculty inherent in man, though we cannot often detect any natural and necessary connection between a particular object and the vocal sound by which this or that people presents it." And he adds: "There can be little doubt that a colony of children, reared without hearing sounds uttered by those around them, would at length form for themselves a speech." Many other citations might be made, showing that philologists have more than once been fairly on the track of the cause to which the origin of linguistic families is due. If they have failed to follow to its conclusion the path into which their intuitions had led them, it has simply been from lack of the evidence now at hand.

In the light of the facts which have now been set forth, it becomes evident that, to insure the creation of a speech which shall be the parent of a new linguistic stock, all that is needed is that two or more young children should be placed by themselves in a condition where they will be entirely, or in a large degree, free from the presence and influence of their elders. They must, of course, continue in this condition long enough to grow up, to form a household, and to have descendants to whom they can communicate their new speech. We have only to inquire under what circumstances an occurrence of this nature can be expected to take place.

There was once a time when no beings endowed with articulate speech existed on this planet. When such beings appeared, whether at one centre or at several, the spread of this human population over the earth would necessarily be gradual. So very slow and gradual, indeed, has it been, that many outlying tracts — Iceland, Madeira, the Azores, the Mauritius, St. Helena, the Falkland Islands, Bounty Island, and others — have only been peopled within recent historical times, and some of them during the present century. This diffusion of population would take place in various ways, and under many different impulses; — sometimes as the natural result of increase and overcrowding, sometimes through the dispersion caused by wars, frequently from a spirit of adventure, and occasionally by accident, as when a canoe was drifted on an unknown shore. In most instances, a considerable party, comprising many families, would emigrate together. Such a party would carry their language with them ; and the change of speech which their isolation would produce would be merely a dialectical difference, such as distinguishes the Greek from the Sanscrit, or the Ethiopic from the Arabic. The basis of the language would remain the same. No length of time, so far as can be inferred from the present state of our knowledge, would suffice to disguise the resemblance indicating the common origin of such dialect-languages. But there is another mode in which the spread of population might take place, that would lead in this respect to a very different result. If a single pair, man and wife, should wander off into an uninhabited region, and there, after a few years, both perish, leaving a family of young children to grow up by themselves and frame their own speech, the facts which have been adduced will show that this speech might, and probably would, be an entirely novel language. Its inflections would certainly be different from those of the parent tongue, because the speech of children under five years of age has commonly no inflections. The great mass of vocables, also, would probably be new. The strong language-making instinct of the younger children would be sufficient to overpower any feeble memory which their older companions might retain of the parental idiom. The natural disposition of the oldest child, indeed, would be to yield to the youngest in this regard. He would feel it to be essential that he should make his little brother or sister understand him, and he would adopt without hesitation any manner of speech that would insure this object. The baby-talk, the " children's language," would become the mother-tongue of the new community, and of the nation that would spring from it.

Those who are familiar with the habits of the hunting tribes of America know how common it is for single families to wander off from the main band in this manner, — sometimes following the game, sometimes exiled for offences against the tribal law, sometimes impelled by the all-powerful passion of love, when the man and woman belong to families or classes at deadly feud or forbidden to intermarry. In these latter cases, the object of the fugitives would be to place as wide a space as possible between themselves and their irate kindred. In modern times, when the whole country

is occupied, their flight would merely carry them into the territory
of another tribe, among whom, if well received, they would quickly
be absorbed. But in the primitive period, when a vast uninhabited
region stretched before them, it would be easy for them to find
some sheltered nook or fruitful valley, in which they might hope
to remain secure, and rear their young brood unmolested by human
neighbors.

If, under such circumstances, disease or the casualties of a hunt-
er's life should carry off the parents, the survival of the children
would, it is evident, depend mainly upon the nature of the climate
and the ease with which food could be procured at all seasons of the
year. In ancient Europe, after the present climatal conditions were
established, it is doubtful if a family of children under ten years of
age could have lived through a single winter. We are not, therefore, surprised to find that no more than four or five linguistic stocks
are represented in Europe, and that all of them, except the Basque,
are believed, on good evidence, to have been of comparatively late
introduction. Even the Basque is traced by some, with much probability, to a source in North Africa. Of northern America, east of
the Rocky Mountains and north of the tropics, the same may be
said. The climate and the scarcity of food in winter forbid us to
suppose that a brood of orphan children could have survived, except possibly, by a fortunate chance, in some favored spot on the
shore of the Mexican Gulf, where shell-fish, berries, and edible
roots are abundant and easy of access.

But there is one region where Nature seems to offer herself as
the willing nurse and bountiful step-mother of the feeble and unpro-
tected. Of all countries on the globe, there is probably not one in
which a little flock of very young children would find the means of
sustaining existence more readily than in California. Its wonderful climate, mild and equable beyond example, is well known. Mr.
Cronise, in his volume on the "Natural Wealth of California," tells
us, that "the monthly mean of the thermometer at San Francisco
in December, the coldest month, is 50°; in September, the warm-
est month, 61°." And he adds: "Although the State reaches
to the latitude of Plymouth Bay on the north, the climate, for its
whole length, is as mild as that of the regions near the tropics.
Half the months are rainless. Snow and ice are almost strangers,
except in the high altitudes. There are fully two hundred cloud-
less days in every year. Roses bloom in the open air through all

seasons." Not less remarkable than this exquisite climate is the astonishing variety of food, of kinds which seem to offer themselves to the tender hands of children. Berries of many sorts — strawberries, blackberries, currants, raspberries, and salmon-berries — are indigenous and abundant. Large fruits and edible nuts on low and pendent boughs may be said, in Milton's phrase, to " hang amiable." Mr. Cronise enumerates, among others, the wild cherry and plum, which " grow on bushes "; the barberry, or false grape (*Berberis herbosa*), a " low shrub," which bears- edible fruit ; and the Californian horse-chestnut (*Æsculus Californica*), "a low, spreading tree or shrub, seldom exceeding fifteen feet high," which " bears abundant fruit, much used by the Indians." Then there are nutritious roots of various kinds, maturing at different seasons. Fish swarm in the rivers, and are taken by the simplest means. In the spring, Mr. Powers informs us, the whitefish " crowd the creeks in such vast numbers that the Indians, by simply throwing in a little brushwood to impede their motion, can literally scoop them out." Shell-fish and grubs abound, and are greedily eaten by the natives. Earth-worms, which are found everywhere and at all seasons, are a favorite article of diet. As to clothing, we are told by the authority just cited that " on the plains all adult males and all children up to ten or twelve went perfectly naked, — while the women wore only a narrow strip of deer-skin around the waist." Need we wonder that, in such a mild and fruitful region, a great number of separate tribes were found, speaking languages which a careful investigation has classed in nineteen distinct linguistic stocks ?

The climate of the Oregon coast region, though colder than that of California, is still far milder and more equable than that of the same latitude in the east ; and the abundance of edible fruits, roots, river-fish, and other food of easy attainment, is very great. A family of young children, if one of them were old enough to take care of the rest, could easily be reared to maturity in a sheltered nook of this genial and fruitful land. We are not, therefore, surprised to find that the number of linguistic stocks in this narrow district, though less than in California, is more than twice as large as in the whole of Europe, and that the greater portion of these stocks are clustered near the Californian boundary.

It is not, however, necessary to suppose that in every instance both parents had perished. If only one of them died, leaving four or five children, — the oldest perhaps not more than six years old, — the surviving parent, having no adult companion to converse with, would infallibly, as a matter of absolute necessity, adopt the language of the children, and to a large extent fall in with their ways of thought. The only difference would be, that when, with the growth of the children in years and intelligence, grammatical inflections came to be gradually developed, these inflections, if not the same as those of the parent's mother-tongue, would probably be of a similar cast. Indeed, this to some extent might be expected, even when both parents had perished. Some reminiscences of the parental speech would probably remain with the older children, and be revived and strengthened as their faculties gained force. Thus we may account for the fact which has perplexed all inquirers, that certain unexpected and sporadic resemblances, both in grammar and in vocabulary, which can hardly be deemed purely accidental, sometimes crop up between the most dissimilar languages. Such are the surprising resemblances between some of the Aryan and Semitic numerals ; and such are the curious concordances between some of the Aryan and the Malayo-Polynesian roots, which perplexed and for a time misled so great a philologist as Bopp. Among languages of the polysynthetic class, few are more unlike than the Algonkin, the Iroquois, and the Dakota ; yet in all three the word for foot is almost identical. This word is *sit*, or, without the terminal consonant, *si* (in English orthography *see*). A word so brief, distinct, and easy of utterance would be likely to survive in the memory of any child of four or five years who had heard it as frequently repeated by the mother as this word would certainly be.

We must also remember that a certain similarity in the form or mould of all idioms spoken by tribes of the same race, even when these idioms originated from such child-languages, would be apt to arise, partly from similarity of character and circumstances, and partly from the inherited conformation of the brain. Of the former class of influences, — the effect of the environing circumstances, first on the character and then on the speech, — we have an elaborate and most suggestive discussion in Mr. Byrne's recent work on the " Principles of the Structure of Language." As regards the inherited powers of mind, we have to consider that when, in any group of children, the faculty of language was strong, their speech would probably develop into a highly complex idiom, like the Aryan, the Semitic, the Basque, or the Algonkin; when this faculty was less powerful, the speech would be simpler, like the Malayan, the Mongol, and the Maya; and when it was very weak, the language would remain, like the Chinese and Anamese, in the monosyllabic or infantile stage. It is proper, further, to bear in mind, that a strong or weak capacity for language does not necessarily imply a corresponding strength or weakness of the other intellectual powers. On this point Professor Whitney, in his " Life and Growth of Language," well observes : " The Chinese is a most striking example of how a community of a very high grade of general ability may exhibit an extreme inaptitude for fertile linguistic development. We may suitably compare this with the grades of aptitude shown by various races for plastic, or pictorial, or musical art, which by no means measure their capacity for other intellectual or spiritual products."

A glance at other linguistic provinces will show how aptly this explanation of the origin of language-stocks everywhere applies. Tropical Brazil is a region which combines perpetual summer with a profusion of edible fruits and other varieties of food, not less abundant than in California. Here, if anywhere, there should be a great number of totally distinct languages. We learn on the best authority, that of Baron J. J. von Tschudi, in the Introduction to his recent work on the " Organism of the Khetshua Language," that this is the fact. He says : " I possess a collection made by the well-known naturalist, Joh. Natterer, during his residence of many years in Brazil, of more than a hundred languages, lexically completely distinct, from the interior of Brazil." And he adds : " The number of so-called *isolated* languages — that is, of such as, according to our present information, show no relationship to any other, and which therefore form distinct stocks of greater or less extent — is in South America very large, and must, on an approximate estimate, amount to many hundreds. It will perhaps be possible hereafter to include many of them in larger families, but there must still remain a considerable number for which this will not be possible."

The explanation which the learned writer gives of this great diversity of languages is that which has been heretofore received by most philologists. "The cause of this remarkable phenomenon," he writes, " is evidently to be found in the subdivision of the Indian population. The evidence of language leads to the conclusion that the separation of families and tribes from the main body of the descendants of the first in-comers must have taken place in very early times. In their wanderings toward the south, the descendants of these straggling hordes must have separated again and again. Many of them may have been brought into positions which were remote from the great lines of migration, may there have remained more or less isolated, may have naturally, in their new relations and surroundings, formed a new vocabulary, and have cast aside and forgotten much of their old speech as useless in their new circumstances. But this forgetting and new-making took place not only in the names given to objects, but in all linguistic expressions as well, including the structure of words and sentences. Languages wholly new arose. Frequently a single family, which broke off from the horde, and moved away in a separate course, has given rise to an entirely new speech." .

If by the phrase " a single family " we could understand such a group of young children as has just been described, this explanation would exactly accord with the view proposed in this paper. This, however, is evidently not the writer's meaning; and, with all due deference to the eminent and justly esteemed author, I may venture to affirm that the process which he describes is opposed to all experience and observation. There is no instance known of a tribe or family of grown-up persons losing their original language in the way he has supposed. The branches of the great Malayo-Polynesian family, scattered over a thousand islands, large and small, from Madagascar to Hawaii, have retained everywhere the mass of their vocabulary and grammar with remarkable uniformity. The thorough analyses furnished by Dr. F. Müller, in his latest work, leave no room for doubt on this point. It is plain that each island has been peopled by one or more canoe-loads of emigrants, bringing their language with them. A still more striking example is to be noted in Australia, where a vast region, larger than Brazil, is found inhabited by hundreds, perhaps thousands, of petty tribes, as completely isolated as those of South America, but all speaking languages of one stock. And if we inquire why many different linguistic stocks have not arisen in that region, as in California, Brazil, and Central Africa, the explanation presents itself at once. Though the climate is as mild as in any of these regions, the other conditions are such as would make it impossible for an isolated group of young children to survive. The whole of Australia is subject to severe droughts, and is so scantily provided with edible products that the aborigines are often reduced to the greatest straits. It is well known that an entire exploring party of white men, well provided with fire-arms, perished of famine in attempting to traverse the interior. The suspicious and unsocial character of the Australian natives, the smallness of their tribes, their wide dispersion, and the little communication between them, are all well-known facts. If linguistic stocks could arise in the way supposed by Herr von Tschudi, there should be hundreds in Australia; but there is only one.

A curious ethnological fact, which tends strongly to confirm the view of the origin of linguistic stocks now proposed, is the circumstance that, as a general thing, each linguistic family has its own mythology. This remarkable fact has been noticed, and well set forth, by Major Powell; and it had, I may add, already occurred to myself in connection with the present inquiry, in which it finds its sufficient explanation. Of course, when the childish pair or group, in their isolated abode, framed their new language and transmitted it to their descendants, they must necessarily at the same time have framed a new religion for themselves and their posterity; for the religious instinct, like the language-making faculty, is a part of the mental outfit of the human race.

But we are now brought face to face with another problem of great difficulty. The view which has just been presented shows that all the vast variety of languages on earth may have arisen within a comparatively brief period; and many facts seem to show that the peopling of the globe by the present nations and tribes of men is a quite recent event. The traditions of the natives of America, North and South, have been gathered and studied of late years, by scientific inquirers, with great care and valuable results. All these traditions, Eskimo, Algonkin, Iroquois, Choctaw, Mexican, Maya, Chibcha, Peruvian, represent the people who preserved them as new-comers in the regions in which they were found by the whites. Ethnologists are aware that there is not a tradition, a monument, or a relic of any kind, on this continent, which requires us to carry back the history of any of its aboriginal tribes, of the existing race, for a period of three thousand years. In the Pacific Islands the recent investigations have had a still more striking and definite result. We know, on sufficiently clear evidence, the times when most of the groups, from New Zealand to the Sandwich Islands, were first settled by their Polynesian occupants. None of the dates go back beyond the Christian era. Some of them come down to the last century. In Australia the able missionary investigators have ascertained that the natives had a distinct tradition of the arrival of their ancestors, who entered by the northwest coast. It is most unlikely that, among such a barbarous and wandering race, a tradition of this nature should be more than two thousand years old. Probably it is much less ancient. We know positively that the neighboring group of New Zealand was settled only about five hundred years ago. Passing on to the old continent, we find that the Japanese historical traditions go back, and that doubtfully, only to a period about twenty-five hundred years ago; those of China, only about four thousand years; those of the Aryans, vaguely, to about the same time; the Assyrians, more surely, a little longer; and the Egyptians to the date fixed by Lepsius for Menes, not quite four thousand years before Christ. No evidence of tradition, or of any monument of social man, points to his existence on the earth at a period exceeding seven thousand years before the present time. Yet the investigations which have followed the discoveries of Boucher de Perthes have satisfied the great majority of scientific men that human beings have been living on the globe for a term which must be computed, not by thousands of years, but by tens and probably hundreds of thousands. Writers of all creeds, and of all opinions on other subjects, concur in the view that the existence of man goes back to a remote period, in comparison with which the monuments of Egypt are but of yesterday; and yet these monuments, as has been said, are the oldest constructions of social man which are known to exist. How shall we explain this surprising discrepancy? How shall we account for the fact that man has existed for possibly two hundred thousand years, and has only begun to form societies and to build cities within less than seven thousand years? In other words, how, as scientific men, shall we bring the conclusions of geology and palæontology into harmony with those of archæology and history?

Fortunately, the geologists and physiologists themselves, by their latest discoveries, have furnished the means of clearing up the perplexities which their earlier researches had occasioned. We learn from these discoveries that, while a being entitled to the name of man has occupied some portions of the earth during a vast space of time, in one and perhaps two geological eras, the acquisition by this being of the power of speech is in all probability an event of recent occurrence. The main facts on which this opinion is based must necessarily, in this summary, be very briefly stated. For other evidences, reference must be made to the sources where they will be found fully set forth.

The question of the existence of man in the tertiary era has been so thoroughly and ably discussed by my predecessor in this office, Professor Morse, in his address at the Philadelphia meeting in 1884, that I need not add a word on that subject. The fact that man existed in the subsequent period, which is known among English geologists as the pleistocene era and in France more commonly as the quaternary age, is questioned by no one. The men of that era, the Palæolithic men, as they are styled, are distinguished by the investigators, as is well known, into two distinct races, belonging to widely different epochs. These races are variously designated by the eminent authorities to whom I shall have occasion to refer, and who, while they differ on some points, are on the the main question of the existence and the distinction of these races fully in accord. These authorities, it may here be stated, are, for France, Prof. de Quatrefages and Prof. G. de Mortillet, and for England, Prof. Boyd Dawkins. The views of M. de Quatrefages are set forth in his work entitled "Hommes Fossiles et Hommes Sauvages," published in 1884, and in his well-known treatise on "The Human Species," of which the eighth edition has appeared during the present year. The work of M. de Mortillet, "Le Préhistorique," appeared in 1883, and that of Prof. Boyd Dawkins, "Early Man in Britain," was published in 1880. Those who had the pleasure of hearing Professor Dawkins at the Montreal meeting of the British Association, in 1884, are aware that his researches subsequent to the publication of that work had only confirmed the views expressed in it. I have also referred to the work of Dr. Paul Topinard, "L'Anthropologie," of which the fourth edition appeared in 1884 ; to the work of Prof. George H. von Meyer, of Zurich, on the "Organs of Speech" (1884), to the monograph of Dr. Robert Baume, of Berlin, on the "Jaw-Fragments of La Naulette and the Schipka Cave" (1884), and the work of Prof. Robert Hartmann, of Berlin, on "Anthropoid Apes," which has just appeared.

Professor Dawkins styles the earlier Palæolithic race the "River-drift men," and the later "the Cave-men." The River-drift men were, in his view, hunters and savages of the lowest grade. In his opinion, the race is now "as completely extinct as the woolly rhinoceros or the cave bear." We have, he considers, no clue to its ethnology; and its relation to the race that succeeded it is doubtful. The Cave-men were of a much higher order, and were especially remarkable for their artistic talents. He is inclined to believe that their descendants survive in the Eskimo; and whether we accept this view or not, we learn from it that, in the opinion of this eminent investigator, the Cave-men were men of the present race. M. de Quatrefages designates the two races from noted localities where their osseous remains were found. The River-drift man is with him the "man of Canstadt," from the place near which the portion of a cranium belonging to this race was discovered; and the Cave-man is the "man of Cro-Magnon," a well-known locality where several skeletons of this race were brought to light. M. de Mortillet draws his designations from the places in which the implements used by the different races are found in their most typical form. The man of the earlier race is with him the "Chellean man," from Chelles, a place in the Department of Seine-et-Marne; while the later is the Magdalenian man, from La Madéleine in the Department of La Dordogne. He makes two intermediate races, the Mousterian and the Solutrean, which Professor Dawkins is inclined to combine with the Magdalenian in a single race, corresponding to his Cave-men. But in one respect M. de Mortillet makes an even stronger distinction than that of Professor Dawkins between the earlier and later races. Professor Dawkins expresses no opinion on the question whether the River-drift men were or were not endowed with the faculty of speech. Prof. de Mortillet is clear that they were not. This view might fairly enough, as will be seen, be based on the pithecoid character of their remains, and the low grade of intellect shown by their implements; but M. de Mortillet finds a remarkable, and, in his opinion, a decisive evidence, in a lower jaw belonging to this race, which was discovered in 1866 in the cave of La Naulette in Belgium. It is only a fragment, but it contains the central curve, or symphysis, forming the chin. In the inner centre of the ordinary human jaw, there is at this curve a small bony projection or excrescence, usually somewhat rough to the touch, which is known to English and American anatomists as the "mental tubercle," or "the genial tubercle." By French writers it is termed the *apophyse géni*, or genial apophysis, and by German authors the *spina mentalis*. These epithets, "mental" and "genial," it may be remarked, are not the common English adjectives with which we are familiar. "Mental" is here derived, not from the Latin *mens*, the mind, but from *mentum*, the chin ; and, in the same way, " genial" in this case is to be referred, not to the Greek γένος, family or kindred, but to γένυς (or its derivative γενειάς), which means in that language the chin or under-jawbone. With this preface, I give in full the author's description of this remarkable relic. The bone is small, and is supposed to have been that of a female. But though small, it is a powerful jawbone. " In fact," he continues, " the essential character of this fossil is its robustness, if I may so express myself. The bone throughout is thick and stocky, and thus approaches much nearer the jaws of anthropoids than those of man. The chin, in lieu of projecting forward beyond the vertical line, inclines backward. It is something intermediate between the man and the monkey. The sockets of the teeth show that the molars, in place of diminishing from the first to the·last, were developed in the opposite way. Finally, in the middle of the inner curve of the jaw, in place of a little excrescence called the ' genial tubercle,' there is a hollow, as with monkeys. We may, then, say that this human relic is the most pithecoid that has yet been found." The inference to be derived from this formation is thus set forth by our author: " Speech, or articulate language, is produced by movements of the tongue in certain ways. These movements are effected mainly by the action of the muscle inserted in the genial tubercle. The existence of this tubercle is therefore essential to the possession of language. Animals which have not the power of speech do not possess the genial tubercle. If, then, this tubercle is lacking in the Naulette jawbone, it is because the man of Neanderthal, the ' Chellean man,' was incapable of articulate speech."

It must not be supposed, from this brief description, that M. de Mortillet imagined that the genio-glossal muscle, the muscle which moves the tongue, and which in fact, as Prof. von Meyer states, contributes most to the form of that member, was lacking in the Chellean man, as it certainly is not lacking in the anthropoid apes. It is not the muscle itself, but the mode of its insertion, which is to be regarded. In the apes and other lower animals, where the tongue is mainly used to aid in taking, masticating, and swallowing food, much less freedom of motion is required for it than in man, for whom its chief use is in the many delicate movements required in framing the elements of articulate utterance. It is for this greater freedom that the insertion of the muscle — or rather of the muscles, for there are two of these — in the genial tubercle or tubercles (for there are also two of these) is required. Or, to speak still more precisely, it should rather be said that it is by the incessant action of the muscles pulling on the bone in these varied movements, that the tubercles themselves must be deemed to have been developed. Such is the explanation given by the able anatomists whom I have consulted on this curious and important point.

It will seem that a single jawbone affords but scanty evidence on which to base so momentous a conclusion. But confirmation has not been wanting. In August, 1880, Professor Maschka found in the Schipka cave, in Northeastern Moravia, among bones of the elephant, rhinoceros, and other animals of the pleistocene era, a fragment of a human jawbone, bearing a remarkable resemblance to that of the Naulette cave. Like the latter, it inclined backward at the chin, being in this respect intermediate between the jaw of the ape and that of the man ; and, as in the Naulette jaw, the genial tubercle was wanting. The two jawbones have been submitted to a most careful and thorough scrutiny and analysis by Dr. Robert Baume, a distinguished writer on dentistry, who has brought out some novel and important points. He shows that, from the great backward inclination of the chin, the jaw must, when the mouth was open, have pressed upon the larynx and closed it entirely, unless the individual to whom the jaw belonged was of a much more prognathous type — or, in other words, had the lower part of the visage much more projecting — than is known in any now existing race. His conclusion is, that there lived in the diluvial or quaternary age races of men who were markedly inferior to the lowest races now existing. His view of the total disappearance of these ancient races, therefore, harmonizes entirely with that of Professor Dawkins.

This view is further confirmed by an examination of all the crania which are believed, on good grounds, to belong to this pristine people. These skulls are not numerous, but they are sufficient in number to characterize a race, and they are all of one cast. The Canstadt skull, the Neanderthal skull, the fragment of the Eguisheim skull and that of the skull found at Brüx in Austria, as well as the skull lately discovered at Podhaba in Bohemia, all belong to this earlier race, and all show the same peculiar characteristics, — namely, a remarkable projection of the superciliary ridges, or the prominences just above the eyes, and an extremely low and receding forehead. What are termed the frontal prominences, that is, the projections of the upper part of the forehead, are entirely lacking. In both these respects the skulls of this race unquestionably approximate to those of the higher order of apes, the orang, the gorilla, and the chimpanzee. Speaking of the Neanderthal skull, in his Lectures on "Man's Place in Nature," Professor Huxley says: "Under whatever aspect we view this cranium, whether we regard its vertical depression, the enormous thickness of its superciliary ridges, its sloping occiput, or its long and straight squamosal suture, we meet with ape-like characters, stamping it as the most pithecoid of human crania yet discovered." But he adds that the cubic capacity of the skull is about seventy-five inches, which is the average capacity given by Morton for Polynesian and Hottentot skulls, while the average capacity of the gorilla skull is only about one third of that amount. Thus it is clear that the Neanderthal skull is that of a man, and not of an ape. But in these ancient crania the greater portion of the capacity is in the posterior part of the skull. The narrowness and depression of the forehead are remarkable, and exceed anything known in the skulls of existing races. The height of the forehead depends, of course, upon the development of the frontal lobe of the brain. The frontal lobe is made up, as regards its height, of three folds, or convolutions, termed by anatomists the first, second, and third frontal convolutions. These convolutions lie one above the other, the third being the lowest. This third convolution is somewhat thicker than the other two, and adds therefore, in general, somewhat more to the height of the forehead than either of the others. Its absence, or almost entire absence, from the brain, would produce just such a depression, or extraordinary flatness, as we find in the foreheads of these ancient skulls. Now it is a remarkable fact, that, while the brain of a monkey is much smaller than that of a man, its general outline is very similar to that of the human brain. As Professor Huxley says, "the brain of a monkey exhibits a sort of skeleton map of man's." Most of the convolutions which are found in the one are present in the other. But there is one remarkable exception. In the lower apes the third frontal convolution is, according to Hartmann, "entirely absent." In the higher or anthropoid apes, it appears, but only in a rudi-

3

mentary form. " Its great development in men," writes Gewährs-mann, " constitutes one of the most marked distinctions between the brains of apes and those of men." This statement has been questioned, as there is some difference of opinion in regard to the analysis of the convolutions ; but Bischoff, the highest authority, confirms it ; and Professor Hovelacque, in an article recently published in the *Revue Scientifique* on " The Evolution of Language," repeats the statement in these significant words : " We mention here, without dwelling upon it, that the faculty of language stands in close relation with a certain one of the frontal convolutions of the brain, which the inferior monkeys do not possess, and which is found in a rudimentary state in the anthropoids, but of which the full acquisition and most complete development have made man what he is, the master of articulate speech."

This third frontal convolution is sometimes called " Broca's convolution," from the fact that the distinguished French physiologist, Dr. Paul Broca, was the first to localize the faculty of language in it. This faculty, according to the description given by Dr. Topinard in his " Anthropology," has its seat in " the posterior portion of Broca's third frontal convolution." " Its surface has a vertical height of about four centimeters " (or a little over an inch and a half), " and an antero-posterior extension of from two to three and a half centimeters," that is, from a little less than an inch to nearly an inch and a half. Any lesion or disease of this part of the brain, as is well known to medical men, produces aphasia, or the loss of the power of speech. If this convolution were absent from the human brain, or were only present in a rudimentary form, as in the anthropoid apes, the man would be incapable of speech, and the height of his forehead would be greatly diminished. We should have, in fact, the precise difference which exists between the frontal portion of the Neanderthal or Podhaba skull, and that of the average skull of the present race of men.

Some eminent writers, and one who may justly be styled pre-eminent, M. de Quatrefages, have sought to show that in modern times skulls similar to those of this ancient race have been met with, and in some cases have belonged to persons of no mean intellectual capacity. In his admirable work on " Fossil Men and Savage Men," he gives pictures of the skulls of St. Mansuy, Bishop of Toul, and of a Dánish gentleman, named Kai-Likké, who took some part in politics in the seventeenth century. These are compared with the Neanderthal skull. The measurements are not given, but their outline, and especially the front view of the Kai-Likké cranium, show a distinct superiority in height to the Neanderthal skull; and we must remember that an ecclesiastic or a politician may have but a scant development of the faculty of language, and may yet gain distinction by other intellectual qualities.

The man of the River-drift, this Canstadt or Chellean man, was widely dispersed over a considerable part of the globe. His presence is known by the peculiar implements, or rather implement, which he fashioned; for in reality, as Prof. de Mortillet shows, he had but one, though this appears in varying shape. It is called, among writers on this subject, by different names. Some speak of it as an axe, others simply as the "drift implement," and M. de Mortillet describes it as "a stone fist." It is, in fact, simply a stone chipped rudely into an ovate or almond-like shape, such as would enable a man to grasp it at one end, and strike with it a more effective blow than he could strike with his naked fist. It could be used in this manner for striking, scraping, or pounding, and, in a rough way, for cutting. There is a singular rudeness in its appearance, which marks at once the low intellectual grade of those who fashioned and used it. Dr. Daniel Wilson, in his work on "Prehistoric Man," has some striking remarks on this subject. He observes (in his third chapter) that the investigator, in examining the earliest palæolithic implements, might imagine that he had "traced his way back to the first crude efforts of human art, if not to the evolutionary dawn of a semi-rational artificer. It is a significant fact," he continues, "that no such clumsy unshapeliness characterizes the stone implements of the most degraded savage races." And he adds, that this essential difference of type "seems to point to some unexplained difference" between the artificers of the two periods. The explanation of this difference, which struck and perplexed this most discerning observer, seems now to be found in the fact that the earlier implements were the production of beings whose minds were in the undeveloped state that must necessarily characterize men who had not yet attained the power of speech. No one will question the justice of Professor Whitney's remark on this point: "The speechless man is a being of undeveloped capacities, having within him the seeds of everything great and good, but seeds which only language can fertilize and bring to fruit; he is potentially the lord of nature, the image of his Creator; but in present reality he is only a more cunning brute among brutes." "A man born dumb," observes Professor Huxley, "notwithstanding his great cerebral mass and his inheritance of strong intellectual instincts, would be capable of few higher intellectual manifestations than an orang or a chimpanzee, if he were confined to the society of dumb associates." We need not therefore be surprised to find that, wherever traces of the River-drift men have been discovered, whether in France, England, Greece, Asia Minor, India, North Africa, or America, these traces, which consist merely of their peculiar implements, are everywhere the same, showing no variety in different regions, and no apparent improvement during the lapse of ages. The drift implements which the fortunate and skilful researches of Dr. Abbott have disclosed in New Jersey are in shape exactly like those which earlier investigators had unearthed from the river-banks of France and England.

In view of these and other discoveries indicating the existence of Palæolithic man in America, and also in view of other facts relating to the fauna of the two hemispheres, M. de Mortillet is decidedly of opinion that during a considerable portion of the early quaternary era a connection existed between Europe and America by way of the Faroe Islands, Iceland, and Greenland. It is well known that such a connection existed during the miocene era. It was broken up in the pliocene age. But, as we know, a vast elevation of land in Europe took place during the Glacial Epoch of the quaternary or pleistocene age. The facts adduced by Professor Boyd Dawkins, in his "Early Man in Britain," show that, if this elevation attained the height of five hundred fathoms, it must have restored the connection between the two continents. He also shows that the elevation did actually reach, at least in the region of the Mediterranean, a height of at least four hundred fathoms. An additional rise of a hundred fathoms in the north, which may well be supposed, would have restored the "great tertiary bridge," and enabled the River-drift man, with the various other animals of his epoch which are found on both continents, to pass from one to the other.

But when the next race, which is styled by M. de Quatrefages the race of Cro-Magnon, appeared, the connection between the two continents had long ceased to exist. The Great Ice Age had passed away, and Europe was assuming its present condition. This race of Cro-Magnon offered, in some respects, the strongest possible contrast to the preceding race of Canstadt, or River-drift men. In physical development it was, to use the expression of this distinguished writer, " a magnificent race." The skull is large and well developed, with a forehead at once wide and lofty. The capacity of one of these crania, according to Broca's measurement, was not less than 1,590 cubic centimeters, which exceeds by 119 centimeters the average size of Parisian skulls of the present day. "Thus," adds M. de Quatrefages, "in this savage, a contemporary of the mammoth, we find all the craniological characters generally regarded as the signs of a great intellectual development." To this may be added, that in the earliest lower jaw of this race which has been discovered the genial tubercle is fully developed. The man of this epoch was a social being, endowed with the faculty of speech. His frontal lobe was large and high, and every convolution of the brain must have existed in unusual size. His intellectual powers corresponded with this development. Of this fact we have the most remarkable and indeed astonishing proof in his works of art, — his pictures engraved on pieces of stone, ivory, and bone, and his sculptures in bone and ivory. His representations of the animals of that period — the mammoth, the reindeer, the elk, the bear, the horse, the urus, the chamois, the whale, the pike, and many others — are most admirable for the artistic skill which they display, and for their evident truth to nature. On this point all observers are agreed. " We recognize in them," writes M. de Mortillet, " the works of a people eminently artistic. In these primitive engravings and sculptures we remark so true a sense of form and movement that it is almost always possible to determine exactly the animal represented, and to perceive the intention of the artist. Some of the works are really small masterpieces." " So natural are the attitudes, so exact the proportions," writes M. de Quatrefages, " that a decorative sculptor of our own days, in treating the same subject, could hardly do better than to copy his ancient predecessor." Dr. Wilson speaks in the highest terms of the " skill and intellectual vigor " manifested in these works of art, and adds the noteworthy remark: " In truth, it is far easier to produce evidences of deterioration than of progress, in instituting a comparison between the contemporaries of the mammoth and later prehistoric races of Europe or savage nations of modern centuries." In short, the evidence is clear and unquestionable, that, while the earliest race, the River-drift men, were in form and intellect the lowest race of human beings that have ever existed, their immediate successors, the Cave-men, or race of Cro-Magnon, must be ranked, in shape and aspect, in cranial development, and in intellectual endowments, among the very highest.

It is proper to observe, that M. de Mortillet and Professor Dawkins make a distinction between the Cave-men and the "Neolithic men," or men of the Polished Stone era, who immediately followed them; and they ascribe the remains of Cro-Magnon to the latter race. M. de Mortillet admits, however, that the people of Cro-Magnon were "evidently descendants of the Magdalenians," or Cave-men, who wrought these works of art; and Professor Dawkins shows that the art-loving Cave-men and the less artistic Neolithic population were at one time contemporaries. It should be added, that the fact that this artistic race lived at the same time with the mammoth, which is now extinct, affords no evidence of its great antiquity. The mammoth was merely a variety of the elephant, differing so little from the existing varieties that some naturalists have refused to consider it a distinct species. It probably became extinct at a quite recent period. Another extinct mammal, the great Irish elk, which was hunted both by the Cave-men and by the Neolithic men, survived down to the Bronze age; and the urus, another animal of the quaternary era, only became extinct a few centuries ago. The Cave-men of Professor Dawkins, the Cro-Magnon race of Prof. de Quatrefages, were really a modern people, — a people of our own age. And the question naturally arises, When did this age, the age of speaking man, commence? The answer will doubtless surprise many persons who have been accustomed to consider the question without regard to the primary and all-important distinction between the two races of men, — the speechless and the speaking race. The former can, no doubt, be traced back to an immense and undefined antiquity. The appearance of the latter dates back probably less than ten thousand years.

We might feel tolerably sure of this fact, as a conclusion of simple reasoning. It is impossible to suppose that a people possessing the intellectual endowments of the Cro-Magnon race would remain long in an uncivilized state, if they were once placed in a country where the climate and other surroundings were favorable to the increase of population and to improvement in the arts of life.

Even in the then rigorous climate and other hard conditions of
Western Europe, they had advanced, as Dr. Paul Broca declares,
" to the very threshold of civilization." What must they have
become in Egypt and in Southern Asia? In point of fact, during
a comparatively brief space of time, ranging from five thousand to
seven thousand years ago, the men of these regions developed in
widely distant centres — in Egypt, in Mesopotamia, in Phœnicia,
in Northern India, and in China — a high and varied civilization
and culture, whose memorials, in their works of art and their literature, astonish us at this day, and in some respects defy imitation.
To what circumstance can we attribute this sudden and wonderful
flowering of human genius, after countless ages of torpidity, but to
the one all-sufficient cause, — the acquisition of the power of speech?
Many skilled observers have sought to discover by various indica-
tions, such as the accumulation of débris in caves, the layers of
earth formed by streams, the growth of bogs, and other evidences,
the time which has elapsed from the era of the Cave-men and the
Neolithic race to our own time. Professor Dawkins, in his account
(given in his work on " Cave-Hunting") of the exploration of the
Victoria Cave, at Settle in Yorkshire, makes an estimate, from the
accumulation of talus in the cave, of the time which has elapsed
since the cave was occupied by Neolithic man, and fixes it at about
4,800 or 5,000 years. Many other investigators have reached similar results. Their conclusions are well summed up by Prof. Alex-
ander Winchell, in his work entitled " Preadamites." "Morlot," he
tells us, " from the study of the layers constituting the ' cone of
the Tinière,' — a deposit formed by a torrent discharging itself into
the Lake of Geneva, — concluded that the Polished Stone epoch
dates back 4,700 to 7,000 years. Gillieron, from researches at the
Bridge of Mièle, is led to fix the epoch of Polished Stone at 6,700
years. Steenstrup, from investigations in the bogs of Denmark, is
led to regard 4,000 years as the minimum for that epoch. De Ferry,
from a study of the river-drifts of the Saône, puts the Polished
Stone epoch at 4,383 years, and the epoch of the mammoth at 5,844
to 7,305 years, — " fortunate," adds Professor Winchell, dryly, " if
the thousands are as exact as the units in these figures." Arcelin,
he further tells us, from a separate study of the drifts of the same
river, arrives at a very close agreement with De Ferry, putting
the epoch of Polished Stone from 3,000 to 4,000 years back, and
the blue clay, containing the mammoth, from 6,700 to 8,000 years.

Finally, Le Hon, in view of all the results, fixes the age of Polished Stone at from 4,000 to 6,000 years, the age of the reindeer (which is in fact the age of Professor Dawkins's Cave-men) at a point beyond 7,000 years, and carries back the age of the mammoth to an indefinite period. All these estimates are in substantial accord; and none of them place the appearance of the Neolithic race, or men of the Polished Stone epoch, earlier than seven thousand years, or that of the Cave-men, or men of the Reindeer period, more than eight thousand years back. The terms in each case are as likely to be less than these numbers as they are to be greater. It is impossible not to yield assent to such a mass of concurrent evidence.

If a pair of human beings, male and female, endowed with speech and possessing the faculties of the earliest known people, the Cro-Magnon race, appeared in some region of the old continent where the climate and the natural productions were favorable to the existence of men, what time would be required for their descendants to become numerous enough to found the early communities of Egypt and Mesopotamia, and to spread into Europe and Eastern Asia? The question is easily answered. Supposing the population to double only once in fifty years, which is a very low estimate, it would amount in twelve hundred years to about forty millions, and in fourteen hundred years would be over six hundred millions, or nearly half the present population of the globe. That less than a thousand years will suffice to create a high civilization, the examples on our own continent presented by the Mexicans, the Mayas, the Muyscas, and the Peruvians amply prove. And that the same space of time would be sufficient for the development of the physical peculiarities which characterize the various races of men, by climatic and other influences, is made clear by the evidence accumulated by Prichard, De Quatrefages, Huxley, and other careful and trustworthy investigators. Nor need the change of climate which was undoubtedly in progress during the earlier part of the existence of the Cro-Magnon race, and which is believed to have contributed to the extinction of the mammoth and other animals of that era, have occupied a longer period. In fact, the observations and estimates just quoted from Professor Winchell seem to show clearly that it did not. If the diversity of languages has had its origin in the cause suggested in this essay, and may therefore have arisen in any period, however brief, during which the peopling of the world has proceeded, there would seem to be no grounds whatever for referring the first appearance of speaking man to a greater antiquity than eight, or at the most ten, thousand years.

How, and where, did this momentous apparition occur? These are questions which naturally arise, and our inquiry would not be complete without a brief consideration of them. That the "speaking man" of our era is a descendant of the "speechless man" of the River-drift period cannot be doubted. We have not to deal with the origin of a new species, but simply with that of a variety. There can be no question that this variety arose in the usual way, by what is termed the process of heterogenesis, or, in other words, the law by which the offspring differs from the parents. As every child has two parents, it cannot resemble both, and, in point of fact, it never exactly resembles either of them. Ordinarily, this unlikeness is restricted within certain defined and rather narrow limits ; but occasionally, as when dwarfs or giants are born to parents of ordinary stature, it is very great. Among the lower animals, when such offspring propagate their like, a new variety or breed arises, which sometimes differs very widely from the original stock, — as occurred, for example, in the Ancon or otter breed of sheep, which thus originated in New England, and in the hornless cattle which have overspread several provinces of Paraguay. That in some family of the primitive speechless race two or more children should have been born with the faculty and organs of speech is in itself a fact not specially remarkable. Much greater differences between parents and offspring frequently appear. Among these, for example, is one so common as to have received in physiology the scientific name of polydactylism, — a term applied to the case of children born with more than the normal number of fingers. M. de Quatrefages mentions that in the family of Zerah Colburn, the celebrated calculator, four generations possessed this peculiarity, which commenced with Zerah's grandfather. In the fourth generation four children out of eight still had the supernumerary fingers, although in each generation the many-fingered parent had married a person having normal hands. Plainly, he adds, if this Colburn family had been dealt with like the Ancon breed of sheep, a six-fingered variety of the human race would have been formed ; and this, it may be added, would have been a far greater variation than was the production of a speaking race descending from a speechless pair. The appearance of a sixth finger requires new bones, muscles, and tendons, with additional nerves leading ultimately to the brain. There is good reason to believe that the first endowment of speech demanded far less change than this. All the anthropoid apes can utter cries of some sort, and some of them can make a variety of sounds. Professor Hartmann expressly informs us that the larynx in these animals resembles in the main that of man. We cannot doubt that our primitive ancestor, the *Homo alalus*, in spite of his name, could utter many sounds, and possessed the usual vocal organs. Professor Huxley has dwelt with much force on the slight anatomical difference which might exist between the speechless and the speaking man. A change of the minutest kind, he tells us, in the structure of one of the nerves which communicate with the vocal chords, or in the structure of the part in which it originates, or in the supply of blood to that part, or in one of the muscles to which it is distributed, might render all of us dumb. And he adds (in words similar to those already quoted) : " A race of dumb men, deprived of all communication with those who could speak, would be little indeed removed from the brutes. The moral and intellectual difference between them and ourselves would be practically infinite, though the naturalist should not be able to find a single shadow even of specific structural difference."

In the actual case, so far as can be judged from the osteology, the changes which took place when the speaking children were born to the speechless pair were in the greater development of the cerebral convolution in which the faculty of language resides, in the new direction given to the under part of the lower jaw, which now projected forward instead of receding, and in the increased volume and strength of the genio-glossal muscles, which by their action developed the genial tubercle, and gave at once greater size and more freedom of movement to the tongue. These changes, though so important in their results, were really slight compared with the changes in a case of polydactylism. The chief alteration was, of course, that which took place in the brain. It was simply the enlargement of a fold of that organ ; but its effect was prodigious, and has transformed the globe. This enlarged fold was the seat, not merely of the faculty of language, but of many other faculties, all of which showed at once the effect of their newly acquired power.

And here it is proper to remark on the mistake, or the confusion of processes, which has led some esteemed writers to suppose that the first speaking men, originating from parents of weak mental capacity, must have partaken of that intellectual feebleness. Elaborate works have been written on this subject, in which the whole argument has been based on the supposition that the earliest of speaking men were inferior to their successors, not merely in accumulated knowledge, — which was a matter of course, — but in mental power, which is a very different affair. The lowest tribes of our time — the Australians, Hottentots, Fuegians, and other savages — have been assumed to be fair representatives of what our earliest ancestors must have been when they were first endowed with the faculty of speech. This supposition is contrary both to reason and to the known facts. It confuses two processes, which are totally unlike in their working and in their results. The changes caused by climate and the other external influences which are commonly known as the "environment" are gradual. The changes which arise from heterogenesis are sudden, and are at once complete. In the cases of polydactylism, we do not find that a mere germ or stump of a finger first appears, and gradually becomes longer and stronger in succeeding generations. The perfect finger appears at once. So in the lower animals: the Ancon or otter breed is known to have sprung from a single sheep, born with abnormally short legs, which became no shorter in its descendants. The hornless cattle of Paraguay are known to be all descended from a single animal, which was born without horns. There is no reason for supposing that the earliest speaking men may not have been endowed with the highest intellectual faculties of the human race. There is every reason to believe that they were so endowed. The race of Cro-Magnon, the earliest known race of social men, though barbarians, were, in point of cerebral development and of artistic powers, not only superior to any barbarians of the present day, but certainly equal, if not superior, to any civilized race that has ever existed. The other earliest communities known to us, those of Egypt and of Southwestern Asia, have surpassed in their architecture and their inventions all succeeding races. Their temples and other structures are the despair of our architects. All the first elements of knowledge and of progress have come from them. They invented pottery and glass, the plough and the loom. They invented the alphabet, and with it a varied and voluminous literature. They invented astronomy, geometry, and history. They smelted copper and iron. They tamed almost all the most useful

animals. They first cultivated almost all the most valuable escu-
lents. They and their earliest offshoots devised all the forms of
settled government, — monarchy in Assyria and Egypt, theocracy
in India, aristocracy in Phœnicia, and democracy in Arabia. They
invented the great Egyptian, Assyrian, and Aryan religions, and
endowed their gods with the qualities of knowledge, power, and justice, which they most admired in their rulers. In Egypt they in-
stituted the judgment after death, and in Assyria they established
the Sabbath. Their period was that which has been well styled by
Mr. Gladstone the " youth of the world," —*juventus mundi*, —
when the human race, on its thinly peopled planet, felt all its ener-
gies called forth to meet the wants and solve the problems of its
new existence.

This conclusion as to the high intellectual grade of the earliest
speaking man is very important in its bearing on our views respecting the so-called inferior races. It is clear that they represent, not
this primitive man, but simply a degeneration caused by unfavorable
influences. If this degeneration has taken place, as there seems
every reason for believing, within a very brief period, — five or six
thousand years at furthest, and most of it probably within a few
centuries after their separation from the original stock, — there
seems good reason for believing that an improvement in their surroundings will be followed by a gradual elevation, and a return to
the high primitive type.

The question of the region in which speaking man first appeared
is one on which there is room for a wide difference of opinion. It
is a question about which no one will venture to dogmatize. The
natural supposition, of course, would be that this first appearance
took place somewhere near the centres of the earliest civilization.
These centres were in Egypt and Assyria. Between those countries lies Arabia, in which, amidst the sandy desert that protects
the land from invasion, there are many oases, large and small,
blessed with a most genial climate and a fruitful soil. In these
oases, which have never known the sway of a foreign conqueror,
the native traditions go back to a dim antiquity, in which no evidence of early barbarism is discerned. From that primitive centre,
if such it was, the increasing population would speedily overflow
into the plains of Mesopotamia and the fertile valley of the Nile;
and there, or in their near vicinity, nearly all the animals which
were first tamed, and nearly all the plants which were first culti-

vated, would be found. We need not be surprised, therefore, to find that the great majority of investigators have looked to South-western Asia for the primitive seat of the human race. The most distinct tradition that has come down to us of the earliest belief respecting the creation of man — the tradition which is preserved in the Hebrew narrative — places it in an oasis on the Arabian border, and dates it apparently at about the time when, as all the evidence seems to show, man endowed with speech first appeared.

One other question, not certainly of the first importance, but still of curious and genuine interest, remains to be considered. If the first language spoken by man was invented less than ten thousand years ago, it may be deemed next to a certainty that this language has survived to our time, — not, of course, in its exact original form, but in some derived idiom. It may be taken for granted that the population speaking this language would be widely diffused, and would have many descendants, now speaking affiliated languages of the original stock. There are three families of languages clustered about the supposed centre of this priscan population, the Hamito-Semitic, the Aryan, and the Ural-Altaic. The Hamito-Semitic stock has for its earliest representatives the Arabic, the Assyrian, the Hebrew, and the Egyptian. The Aryan family numbers among its most ancient members the Sanscrit, the Zend, and the Greek. The Ural-Altaic stock, to which the Turkish, the Finnish, and the Hungarian languages belong, finds its chief, but sufficient, claim to high antiquity in the Accadian, whose discovery and decipherment, from the hieroglyphics of the Assyrian inscriptions, have furnished one of the most notable triumphs of modern scholarship. Each of these three great families of speech is very widely diffused, and each of them might advance strong claims to this curious genealogical distinction of being the direct representative of the earliest tongue. The question is one whose determination by strictly scientific methods does not seem by any means beyond reasonable hope. If science can weigh the planets, can define the chemical components of the fixed stars, and describe the shape of continents that existed millions of years ago, it may surely be expected to find evidence for determining the particular linguistic stock to which the earliest spoken language belonged. Such evidence as we have at present certainly seems to favor the Hamito-Semitic family. This family possesses the most ancient literature, and, if the difference between the Hamitic and Semitic groups is considered, seems to

have varied, in the long lapse of ages, most widely. Lepsius and
F. Müller have traced its influence far into the interior of Africa;
and Professor Gerland, going further still, unites the whole population of that vast peninsula with the Semitic group in one great
Arabic-African race. There is a certain evidence — not perhaps
decisive, but worthy of consideration — which seems to connect
the Cro-Magnon race with the Hamitic branch of this family. The
extinct population of the Canary Islands, the Guanches, are known
to have belonged to this Hamitic branch, and their crania, as Prof.
de Quatrefages shows, bear a striking resemblance to those of the
men of the Cro-Magnon era. This cautious investigator does not
hesitate to pronounce the Guanches to be evidently the descendants
of that ancient race. He declares that " the resemblance of cranial
forms sometimes amounts to identity," and he adds the confirma-
tory fact, that a late observer, M. Verneau, has found among the
present islanders — who are in part descended from the Guanches
— implements precisely like those which were used in France by
the Cro-Magnon hunters.

The conclusions to which this inquiry, guided by the most recent
discoveries of science, has directed us, may be briefly summed up.
We find that the ideas of the antiquity of man which have pre-
vailed of late years, and more especially since Lyell published his
notable work on the subject, must be considerably modified. No
doubt, if we are willing to give the name of man to a half-brutish
being, incapable of speech, whose only human accomplishments were
those of using fire and of making a single clumsy stone implement,
we must allow to this being an existence of vast and as yet undefined duration, shared with the mammoth, the woolly rhinoceros,
and other extinct animals. But if, with many writers, we term the
beings of this race the precursors of man, and restrict the name of
men to the members of the speaking race that followed them, then
the first appearance of man, properly so styled, must be dated at
about the time to which it was ascribed before the discoveries of
Boucher de Perthes had startled the civilized world, — that is, somewhere between six thousand and ten thousand years ago. And this
man who thus appeared was not a being of feeble powers, a dull-
witted savage, on the mental level of the degenerate Australian or
Hottentot of our day. He possessed and manifested, from the
first, intellectual faculties of the highest order, such as none of his
descendants have surpassed. His speech, we may be sure, was

not a mere mumble of disjointed sounds, framed of interjections and of imitations of the cries of beasts and birds. It was, like every language now spoken anywhere on earth by any tribe, however rude or savage, a full, expressive, well-organized speech, complete in all its parts. The first men spoke, because they possessed, along with the vocal organs, the cerebral faculty of speech. As Professor Max Müller has well said, "that faculty was an instinct of the mind, as irresistible as any other instinct." It was as impossible for the first child endowed with this faculty not to speak, in the presence of a companion similarly endowed, as it would be for a nightingale or a thrush not to carol to its mate. The same faculty creates the same necessity in our days ; and its exercise by young children, when accidentally isolated from the teachings and influence of grown companions, will readily account for the existence of all the diversities of speech on our globe.

If the views now presented shall be confirmed by further investigations, they will serve to clear up uncertainties which have perplexed the minds of students of linguistic science and of archæology, and have seriously impeded the progress of all the anthropological sciences. The views, with the evidence which seems to sustain them, are therefore respectfully submitted to the candid consideration of the members of our Section, and through them to the students of those sciences in other countries, in the hope of inducing further inquiry which may lead to decisive and satisfactory conclusions on these important questions.